To Li'l 'Mo'

Full of sweetness and joy and peace,
Love is a gift from above,
While the years seem to fly
none can deny
That time alone strengthens true love.

From SMURF.--Xmas,2002

Rhymes of Romance
Poems of Passion

Rhymes of Romance
Poems of Passion

Poetry of love, life and social commentary

Robert E. Kogan

toExcel

New York   San Jose   Lincoln   Shanghai

Rhymes of Romance Poems of Passion
Poetry of love, life and social commentary

Published by toExcel,
an imprint of iUniverse.com, Inc.

For information address:
iUniverse.com, Inc.
620 North 48th Street
Suite 201
Lincoln, NE 68504-3467
www.iUniverse.com

ISBN:1-58348-558-9

Printed in the United States of America

∾ Contents

Poems of Humor and Protest ⌣

Poems of Tribute ⌐

Poems of Life, Nature, Hope and Death ⌐

To all my Internet poet friends with special thanks

To Pamela, who started the dream
To Fay, who shared my dream
To Linda, who tolerated my dream
To Jaine, who promoted my dream

and to

RC, Julie, Lisa and David
Joshua, Noah and Sam

∾ *Foreword*

In this volume of poetry, Robert E. Kogan opens a window to a powerful phenomenon–the resurgence of poetry outside the academy among those who love it, read it–and write it. Skillful, direct, and never pompous, this is public poetry written by a people's poet (a modern–day Walt Whitman) who writes not for university publication, scholars, and classrooms–traditional bastions of poetry in the United States—but for other lovers of language and fellow crafters of verse. Clearly, a great difference between Walt Whitman's time and our own (and Walt would relish this fact) is the powerful presence of the Internet and the speed with which new poems and even chapbooks can circulate "people's poetry" to huge numbers of people.

But Walt Whitman would also see that Robert E. Kogan's work is poetry that heeds his warning—and that of a later poet, William Carlos Williams. Both poets remind us sternly, every chance they get, that if poetry at times seems superfluous, a mere pleasant pastime, a filler for idle hours, make no mistake about it—men and women die every day for lack of what they could find in poetry. That is, people's lives fail constantly and they die for lack of connection with the deeper chords in experience and the palpable significance in life that makes living worth living.

As Robert E. Kogan's poetry shows, these connections continue to be the products of poetry (much as they are the products of religion and philosophy), and whatever we may think about the richness of the information revolution, we still cannot live without deeper knowledge about ourselves and our lives–news that will always strike us as "new" and terribly "old" at the same time.

Whitman and Williams would read Robert E. Kogan's poems and be very happy to see that such crucial knowledge can still come from poetry and that poetry as a form is still a part of our essential lives.

The most dramatic indication of Robert E. Kogan's success in striking these chords is his dialogue poems–and the love relationship, really—between Emily Dickinson and Mr. Kogan's own poetic persona.

These are searching poems that ask about the limits of making sense of our lives, deaths, and disappointments, what Mr. Kogan calls "The grief of want and grief of cold." These are poems that do not respect the usual formulations of "optimism" and "pessimism"–and the frequent shallowness of attitude that those overused words can stand for. Rather, "Emily" and "Robert" dance around each other to explore the far reaches of pleasure and pain and try to determine exactly what of such distant experiential lands can be brought back and embodied for others in poetry. As Emily's companion (lover? fellow poet?), "Robert" has the last word in this exploration and dance when he intones,

No need to cherish death.
So why seek martyrdom?
When all you have to do is live,
For death will surely come.

Be jealous of the living,
And of the life they led–
Celebrate each new tomorrow
When praying for the dead.

This is a poetic voice that has surely learned from Emily Dickinson, but possibly has gone beyond her as well. This is not a voice and perspective tortured by being stranded between the bounds of life and death, as Emily so often was. This a voice and a set of attitudes that recognizes that the "dead," whatever they mean to us, are a legacy of our common lives and that, above all else, at whatever cost, we must "Celebrate each new tomorrow"—the possibility of life.

Finally, as Walt Whitman also taught us, the people's poets are the wise poets and the ones we dare not neglect to read. Because they know our lives, both the nick of time and the deeper chords that move us, perhaps better than anyone else—sociologist, psychologist, or philosopher—they really know us and where we need to direct our attention.

The cumulative testimony of Robert E. Kogan's poetry concerns love—both the necessity and the tremendous cost of loving, each other and ourselves. This is complex, nuanced poetic testimony, and in an era of sound bytes and channel–surfed "love connections," this is "old" news, but old news that we dare not ignore or fail to find the newness in it. Not only will the failure to hear this message surely kill us, as Whitman and Williams knew, but the opportunity opened by such poetic witnessing has power that we must—at whatever cost—continually re–teach ourselves to appreciate.

Robert Con Davis–Undiano
Executive Director, World Literature Today

❧ Introduction

If you asked several poets or writers of fiction why they write, each would tell you in his or her own words that the drive to write is motivated in large part by a deep desire to communicate. Connection to others, social and developmental psychologists tell us, is a basic human need. Writers may feel this need more acutely than others, and the need for connection and for recognition of common experience with others is a driving force for many writers. Whether the work is evidently autobiographical or not, the writer always draws on personal experiences, emotions and encounters, and in a way that can be painfully truthful, owns them. It is only after that "owning" that clear and powerful communication can occur.

Just as the *Velveteen Rabbit* became real as he was loved, what is written becomes more "real" for the author as it is shared.

In offering this collection of my poems, I wanted to connect and make real what drives me. Poetry has been a part of my life since an eighth-grade English class assignment, when, at the age of fourteen, *The Rhyme of the Ancient Mariner* and *The Raven* first revealed to me the musical power of words. Although I have no talent for music, and singing is a challenge friends and family discourage me from, the power of music to evoke strong feelings and emotions has been powerful for me throughout my life. Poetry is a medium that satisfies my desire for music and gives release to my own creativity. In *War* and *Marmenoul*, some of my earliest poems, a lyrical quality is strongly evident, and purposeful. I wanted to make music, and share the music I felt in my soul.

These were some of my first experiences with improvisation. With no idea what I would write a line or two later, no idea of what would follow, I was, like the reader, following a trail of words to where it would end. Words just came, flowing effortlessly, like the rhythm of a waterfall, the rhythm of my heartbeat.

As a young man, I was most productive when I lived in Bucks County, Pennsylvania. With greener–than–possible grassy meadows nestled in rolling mountains, Bucks County was and still is a natural magnet for writers and artists. At that time in my life, most of my friends were artists, and just being around creative people seemed to increase my own creative desires and abilities.

Over the next 25 years, however, the demands of my professional career as a mental health administrator significantly diminished my creative drive and ability. I felt like the proverbial Pogo: I had met the enemy, and it was me. Although the stream of my writing and creative thinking had gone dry, like the secret poetry book I kept in the top drawer of my desk, it was there still, reduced to a trickle deep beneath the surface, but still there. So the majority of the poems in this collection were written after my retirement from professional administrative life in 1995. More than half of my poetry is written in rhyme, the remainder in free-verse. My preferred style is to combine in one poem both aspects, like the rapids and still pools in one stream.

I am often asked why I write so much love poetry. As I said earlier, the essence of poetry is to communicate feelings and emotions. In my life I have been fortunate to feel and experience many different manifestations of love—love of family, love of friends, love of religion, love of knowledge, love of community, and the elusive love of self. In writing poems of love, I looked into and held out a gentle mirror of words, words to reflect all the intense feelings and the many facets of love, the pulse of human life. This intensity and range of feelings are expressed in the poem *Love Is.*

One purpose of my writing is to enable the writer to feel the same emotions I felt while I was writing a particular poem. If I have been successful, if we can share a common experience, then we have truly communicated, waded in the same waters, heard the same melodies, lived our lives as connected parts of the same whole.

Robert E. Kogan, August 1999 Norman, Oklahoma

~ *Love* ~

∾ My Shadow

The shadow of your words
Follows close behind me
Attached to every step my mind now takes.
They're longer in the early morning,
When walking in the sunlight.
When night approaches, your words give light
reflecting back thoughts of memories.
Even at mid–day sun I can see them,
Barely visible underneath my feet.

No voices to distract me,
Your words are company enough.
How quickly the day passes.
I know that they are now my shadow,
For when I reach down to hold them,
They are unable to feel my touch,
And although I try, I cannot pick them up.

Wear Me

I want you to wear me comfortably,
        as you would a dress,
        or the silver necklace that you wear
        around your neck.
Comfortably, so that I am always
        next to you.
But most important—
Something you decide
        each morning to select.

∾ *Your Thoughts*

I have been so busy loving you
That I forgot your thoughts are not my own.

Our feelings move at different speeds,
With different wants and different needs.

And while we loved within my mind—
I may have left your thoughts behind.

~ I'm Not In Love

It's hard to write much any more.
I'm not depressed or blue.
And politics are such a bore.
I'm not in love with you.

I have no Cause to write about.
I have no need to preach or shout—
There is no thought that's fresh or new.
I know I'm not in love with you.

There are no songs I want to hear—
No music ringing in my ear.
Do you still hear that music too?
I know I'm not in love with you.

Remember how we used to talk
The day and all night through?
Remember where we used to walk?
I'm not in love with you.

Sometimes my dreams are almost real—
You are so close that I can feel—
If only dreams could all come true.
I know! I'm not in love with you.

And every day it's all the same—
Each time I talk I speak your name—
I wonder if you miss me too?
Why does it hurt—this loving you?

∼ Within My Mind

Within my mind I've placed you in a shrine
A pedestal, where you have merged with me.
When I sleep, it's your eyes that close, not mine.

We are as one. Our hearts and souls combine.
And thoughts of love are all that I can see.
Within my mind I've place you in a shrine.

But still, your spirit I shall not confine.
A butterfly must soar, must be set free—
When I sleep, it's your eyes that close, not mine.

Within my thoughts, I see you as divine.
I seek no other source for company.
Within my mind, I've placed you in a shrine.

You are dawning ray of day's sunshine.
And at day's end, your starlight comforts me.
When I sleep, it's your eyes that close, not mine.

It is your hand, not mine that touches me.
It is your lips, not mine, that are lonely.
Within my mind, I've placed you in a shrine.
When I sleep, it's your eyes that close, not mine.

If I Were to Suddenly Die Tomorrow

If I were to suddenly die tomorrow,
I would not want my soul
      to travel where most souls go.
Instead I would ask for a temporary
      leave of absence,
Have my soul join yours,
And be your companion until
      we could both take leave together,
      and together share eternity.
Inside of you, I could touch every atom
      that comprises you.
Thank them for the work of art
      they hold together,
For the beauty they enabled,
For the vision they provided,
Allowing me the gift of loving you.

◦ The Garden

There are flowers in the garden,
Watered daily by passing lovers' tears.
Slowly each of the flowers
Begins its growth, and what once were buds,
Opens to reveal the splendor of their beauty.
        Cast their fragrance to the wind.
Yet each individual flower
Is incapable of witnessing its own beauty.
Each individual flower can never view
        the majesty of its own colors.
And one day, come the Autumn,
        each petal slowly begins to fall.
The last thing the flower remembers
is the sadness of what it feels—its own inadequacy.
If only they could have seen themselves
Through the distance view of gentle eyes.
If only they could have inhaled
The fragrance of their own beauty,
They never would have doubted…
If only they could feel the joy
That they have given others,
There would no longer be a need for sadness.
They would shed their petals willingly
With the knowledge they had value.
And their awareness of their splendor
Would eagerly await
The coming of the spring—
When they will flower once again,
And their Nobility will be picked and placed tenderly…
Within the loving hands of God.

Fly Away

Once I loved a rock
Whose heart was set in stone.
And my love was never able to enter,
To rest and find a home.

So I sought love where I found beauty
And a heart crying out to me.
A butterfly to lift my spirits—
Her soul soared free among the clouds;
And then she came, and rested next to me.

It's hard to love a butterfly.
Her soul must fly throughout the sky—
Praising God, who set her free,
And sadly watching, never wanting
To see her fly away from me.

❦ My Fountain Pen

Some men seek your flesh,
Another game to win,
While I seek
To touch your thoughts,
And love you
With my fountain pen.

∾ We Never Had A Chance

There never was a time
When I could hold you—
                    Call you mine.
And all that I can ever do
Is dream these thought I have of you.
Recreate a different past
Where our love would always last.
I never even had a chance
To ask you for the final dance,
Play foolish games and pantomime
Or read to you my latest rhyme.
No memories of joy or bliss,
Or eyes that closed on our first kiss.
We never walked on beach or sand,
Or gently held each other's hand.
We never had a favorite song,
To comfort us the whole night–long.
We never made a perfect team,
We never shared a lover's dream.
For there never was a time
When I could hold you—
                    Call you mine.

Another Morning

If I cannot stop the sun from rising,
The morning sky both red and blue—
If I can't prevent each morning coming,
How can I prevent my wanting you?

I can't control the noon–day sunshine,
Its warmth taking away the dew—
If I can't prevent the earth from turning,
How can I prevent my wanting you?

If I can't control the night time coming,
The stars and moon for me to view—
While loving you the whole day through,
How can I prevent my wanting you?

✎ Give and Take

Taking is making our ego waking,
Enslaving us both from the start.
Demanding a love we both never felt,
Possessing, not loving, your heart.

Love is giving, never taking,
Sharing my soul and my heart.
Love is receiving, never demanding,
The love you returned from the start.

ᑐ Sunday

It is another day,
Only we call this one Sunday.
The day that God decided
       that He needed rest.
At the very beginning of time,
       when all of the souls were created,
When God had given your soul His breath,
He was pleased
       and only then took His long–needed rest.
You could have come here
       at any time or age.
You could have selected the time
       when all the classic art was painted;
You could have selected the age
       when the birth of art began;
But now is when you chose to come.
Knowing that I needed you—
Knowing that my love contains
       the very essence of the art
       you have dreamed about.

Monday

It is just another day,
Only we call this one Monday.
The first day of the week
>for the work force of America
>and the sound of the grinding wheels
>of industry are our alarm clocks.
>Time for haste, no time to waste.
>Never time for love.

The sounds that I hear waking me
>are a gentle purring;
>As you sleep slightly stirring,
>For you still have two more hours
>>left to sleep.
Two hours from now I will send you
>a light kiss, for my passion is
>at rest beginning with daybreak
>and seeks only to kiss away your sleep.
The Wall Street tapes have already
>started their endless movement
>buying and selling like so many lovers do.

The love I send accumulates no interest,
>although its value forever changes
>daily setting new records
>for the length of time
>that I have worshiped you.

❧ Tuesday

It is just another day,
Only this one we call Tuesday.

Another day of gratitude
Another day of prayer
Another day to feel your closeness
Another day to share.

Another day of wanting
To touch your long black hair,
Another day of worship
Knowing you are there.

Your arms have finally reached me.
Showing that you care.

∾ Wednesday

It is just another day,
Only this one we call Wednesday.
Wednesday's child is full of woe,
And I have courted her.
I played with her when she was young,
    and all the games we played were sad.
The game I learned the best was Tears,
    for she taught me how to cry.
When growing up she told me
that you would never come,
    And I learn to taste the loneliness of tears.

When growing older she said
    that you would never come,
And I learned the bitter taste of tears.

She left me when I grew too old,
    I had no tears to give.
    No hope to cry was left.

Then, quite unexpectedly you entered.
    Softly, gently,
    you told me you were here.

Now I cry again
    for wasted tears of youth
    and happiness,
    now that you are near.

～ Thursday

This is not another day,
This day we call birthday.
I celebrate all day today,
As if it were my own.
Place flowers in the shrine I built
In honor of your love.
It is a golden temple
With gates that never lock,
Opening into a garden
Where marble statues face your shrine
And fountains wash away your tears.
There are flowers growing in this garden,
Thirty-nine sections reflecting your every mood.
And by each section, a bench to sit and watch
Your love, making all the flowers grow.
Never once have I entered the Shrine,
For there is far too much beauty inside,
And I need more time to prepare myself
To feel and touch the love within.

Friday

It is another day,
this one we call Friday.
A day of great anticipation,
As week's end approaches.
Time for fun and play, for gaiety—
A tapestry of expectations are woven
  into each plan.
Friday work is laid to rest,
And lovers prepare to spend their weekend
    Seeking pleasure from their wanting
    Seeking comfort in their sharing
    Seeking to live their pleasant dreams.
Fridays represent such fulfillment
To everyone but me.
My fulfillment lies far deeper
Than a Friday night of pleasure.
For I am nourished by her caring
Her giving and her sharing
The comfort she provides to me.
Her compassion is her passion
She gives me more than just her love
The gift she gives me endlessly
Contains her spirituality.
It is the ultimate of love.

❧ Saturday

It is just another day,
Only this one we call Saturday.
The ending of another week.
The beginning of another day—
      growing together.

I saw a painting of two trees
Growing next to one another.
They were so close
their deepest roots
became gently intertwined.
And as years passed,
both separate trees
      united into one.

Eyes could not differentiate
Even God looked down and found
That in this process called Creation
He had created only one.

Now our hearts so softly blend,
We are now, together, one.

My Castle

Once I built a castle
and created many different rooms
so that Love would never tire
    and leave me.

I wanted Love to stay within my castle.
So I slept in a different room each night,
Waiting for Love to come and comfort me,
Waiting for Love to hold me close and tight.
In every room where I placed a bed,
Love must have left when I fell asleep at night,
For there was no Love resting in my arms come morning—
No Love with me to greet the morning light.

Only empty rooms can now be found within my castle.
Each and every room is now the same.
I could not keep Love locked inside my castle.
And now, come morning or night, when I call out,
Only blank walls now respond, and echo back her name.

~ Childish Thoughts

As a child, when you felt joy
Your heart would beat much faster.
Every fiber of your being
Was reflected through your laughter.

And when you felt a need to cry
At such a tender age,
Your body shook in protest
And your fists were clinched in rage.

For you had not yet learned
To hide and to conceal
The needs that you possessed,
And all that you could feel.

And part of me remains a child,
For I have feelings too.
My body, spirit, heart and soul
Cannot help but love you.

∾ Midsummer Parting

It was in the mid part of the summer
When we sat and I told how I lied.
It was in the mid part of the summer
When we kissed to a love that had died.

Remember the eve of that summer
When the stars seemed to kindle the sky,
And the radiant glow that was given
Was ashen and dimmed in your eye?

For trust and belief were then broken
Sorrow and hurt took its place.
Disdain and a coldness was showing
On your saddened, yet much wiser face.

Yet there were two questions you asked me:
Was all that I told you untrue?
Did I lie when I said that I loved you?
But I never answered those two.

How could I tell you we're parting;
Would journey farther away?
If I confessed and said yes, I still love you?
For parting is harder that way.

It was in the mid part of the summer
When we sat, you by my side,
I thought of the sadness of parting
When we kissed to a love that had died.

~ Seasons of Love

In every song,
    there is a season.
There is a reason
    for all we do.
My love has different seasons
    Time enough to worship you.

Spring is where life begins:
The Seasons cycles start anew.
I have experienced my rebirth,
    I have discovered you.

Summer is the time of beauty,
Love is felt the whole day through,
We grew and now we bind together,
    For now, I know, you love me too.

Fall will be that promised harvest,
When we can love the whole night through
Pledging mutual allegiance,
    Angels blessed my loving you.

Winter's chill approaches,
The season's growth is through
I take leave to thank my Maker,
    Allowing me to worship you.

✒ Knocking

Who is that knocking at my front door?
Is it the many lives I lived before?
Is it all my hopes, my dreams,
    my prayers answered?
Or just the wind creating memories?

Must this become another dream?
Another sound of my invention?
Have my tears sought so much beauty unanswered
that the sound is them dropping on the floor?

Is it possible that this sound,
This knocking at my door,
Is the last sound that I shall hear
Before my soul is homeward bound?

Or is it you, all I have wanted,
Searched for all my years?

When I opened the door in my youth,
The sound looked back and laughed at me.
Is it wrong to hope, to pray,
That it is really you come knocking?

I fear that if I open the door
The sound, and you, will disappear.

∾ Love Is

Love is like a river that flows into the sea
Oceans of emotions that form a symphony—
Longing, yearning, hurting, seeking company—
To sing a lovers song in two part harmony.

Love is the promised vision when sight itself is blind—
For where love is found,
                    pain is sure to follow close behind.
Love is always changing; it evolves and grows
Becoming both the flower, and the thorn upon the rose.

Love lasts forever regardless of how brief.
For hearts are filled with wonder and with grief.
Recall each precious moment
                  of the wonder of its starting,
And the sadness felt deep inside
                  when the time came for its parting.

As minutes become days and as days become our years
Love becomes a lesson that our mind and spirit hears.
As an infant becomes a child,
                  and as the child begins to grow,
Love becomes the river in which our feelings flow.

∼ There Is A Time

There is a time for everything,
At least there seems to be.
And Ours was twenty years ago—
That's how it seems to me!

Perhaps if only we had met
When we were young, back in the past
And had we met and fell in love,
That love today would still hold fast.

Our yesterdays have gone.
We missed Our only chance
To meet and fall in love
Experience pure romance.

Today is not the time or place
To wear a lover's hat,
And feel the joy that lovers feel.
Put out the welcome mat!

There are a dozen reasons why
Today it would be wrong
To want to kiss like lovers kiss
And sing a lover's song.

Today we must deny these thoughts,
Fight love with all our might.
But 'way down deep inside of me
My God!—it felt so right!

Time

Time moves swiftly through revolving doors,
Trying desperately to make each moment part of the past.
Oh that time could just stand still
And prevent today from becoming another yesterday.

A new and exciting world awaits us,
One where we could return to youth
And see a glimpse of freshness
And marvel at the wonders around us
If only we had the time.

If our eyes were not so stale,
A three-ring circus would be ours to enjoy
And later, when we grew up, we could walk along the beach
Hand in hand
Forever.
Seeing everything for the first time,
And even Peter Pan would not object to having strings attached
If it were not for the lack of time.

Time moves swiftly through revolving doors,
Trying desperately to make each moment part of the past.
Oh that time could just stand still
And prevent today from becoming just another memory.

∿ *Superfluous Communication*

Writing to you is like walking on eggshells.
I must weigh the meaning of each word I write.
Praying my comma should not be a period,
For that alone would give you reasons to fight.

If I say I miss you and need you today
You will ask me why I am feeling so good.
You get angry when I ask what you're doing.
Whatever I say will be misunderstood.

I write about weather and meals that I eat,
But must never write about feeling distress,
For you sit and wait with great expectation
To pounce on real thoughts that I need to express.

So the weather is fine and I'm feeling great
Not a care in the world—just happy today.
Hope you have fun with the work you are doing
And of course, hope that you are feeling OK.

⮎ *Modern Math*

One,
Trying to become two,
Thinking of you.
Sharing is impossible
When there is only one.
Caring is absurd
Without another one.
But then came you,
And now we are two.
Two, loving as one.
The caring and sharing
have begun.
Two,
Trying to become one.
Isn't it fun?

Humor
and
Protest

❧ *Sensorium*

Red of desire,
Black of the night,
Orange of the fire,
A world to ignite,
    This was the color of passion.

The odor of ashes,
Rust and charred wood
Fill the deep gashes
Where cities once stood.
    This was the smell of hate.

The hunger of nations,
A thirst of greed
Excrete indignations
On which to feed—
    This was the taste of madness.

The winds softly speak
Of yesterday's worth.
Where are the meek
To inherit the Earth?,
    This is the touch of fate.

~ In my Humble Opinion

Yes. Make a big fuss over me,
For I am published. Universities
Have offered me a Chair.
Pay every humble homage due
To every word I write; and yes,
Go right ahead and stare.
I see the worship in your eyes
That my very name inspires—
Of course you care; of course you sigh.
Someday it will come to you,
If you copy all I do, proclaiming,
"There, but for the grace of You, go I."

～ Just Another Inpatient Day in a Ward in Pennsylvania

I first met her when the police escorted her
to the nursing station, handcuffed and accompanied
by an Emergency Order for Detention signed by the
arresting officer when he placed her in protective
custody.

She was in her mid twenties, and had made numerous
suicide attempts since early adolescence. She
had scars on her wrists where she had tried before,
and the saddest, yet most beautiful, eyes I had ever seen.

She was very young when her Father killed himself,
but not so young that she could not remember. The
only thing she forgot was the years before when he
had raped her so frequently it became one long rape
instead of something that happened daily.

And it was a year ago October when her brother
shot himself on the lawn outside of the mental
health center. He was not a patient, but he must
have thought his dying there would be message enough.

She was placed on suicide watch, and for three days
was subject to constant observations. But she was
bright, and knew all the right words to say that would
please her doctors.
After supper on the fourth day she went into the
bathroom and hanged herself from the metal bar which
stretched across the entrance to the toilet to
give her privacy and dignity. Even back then, civil
rights were always a requirement.

Later, after the ambulance left, I found her note
inside the drawer of her bedside table:

> *Please throw away all my clothes,*
> *And all that you might find,*
> *No one will want these ugly things*
> *That I have left behind.*

> *I've tried to be considerate,*
> *You'll have no mess to clean;*
> *No blood to dirty up your floor—*
> *I'm not that bad or mean.*

> *I only have one last request.*
> *I beg you to permit*
> *That my remains be flushed—*
> *With all the other shit.*

She was buried two days later
next to her father and her brother.

∼ If Only I Were ...

If only I were Irish
Then I would have a Cause
And gladly give my life
        and die.

If only I were British,
Then I would have a Cause
And gladly give my life
        and die.

If only I were Asian,
Then I would have a Cause
And gladly give my life
        and die.

If only I were American
Then I would have a Cause
And gladly give my life
        and die.

And if I were but white or black
Arab or Jew, Greek or Turk
Red or Pink or Green
Or Christian, Moslem, Buddhist Priest
Or even somewhere in between
Then I would certainly have a Cause
And die, and die, and really dig the scene.
But I am just a human being
And afraid that if I get involved with that
It will really excite me
And just when I begin to expound my Cause

And say it's great to love and be
By then I'll be alone,
    for everyone will have already
    done their thing.

The Seeker

I am a student,
A seeker of truth.
I yearn for new knowledge each day.
I open my mind,
Which is more than most can,
And seek someone to show me the way.

However, those I find
Have limited minds,
Filled with dogma, rubbish and such.
Whatever limited truth they might have
Certainly won't help me much.

Because I am kind
And pity the small,
I feel sorry for all that I see.
This poor, insignificant, bigoted bunch
Had better start learning from me.

Because I am great,
And because I am wise
I know that there never will be
A more humble, sensitive, misunderstood
Example for mankind than me.

For I am a student,
A seeker of truth.
I yearn for new knowledge each day.
I open my mind
Which is more than most can,
To find someone to show me the way.

~ The Year of the Great Suffering

I remember as a child
    the day the B29's bombed Japan
    and then, from Tinian, the future deliverance
    wrecked havoc on Nagasaki,
For that was the year of the Great Suffering.

I remember Korea, Israel, Egypt,
    Ireland, Vietnam,
    and the agony of the dying
    and the agony of the tears,
For that was the year of the Great Suffering.

I remember the cold, dark and windy skies of Dallas,
    and then Robert, and then Martin
    and the desolation of the people
    and the hurt and disillusionment,
For that was the year of the Great Suffering.

I remember Biafra and the starving,
    Iran, Iraq and Desert Storm,
    and the Trade Center today still trading—
    and Oklahoma City and the children—
    The children who died so quickly
    They still are laughing and still playing,
For that was the year of the Great Suffering.
And today, waiting for fulfillment
    of prophecy from all the written scripture
    before The Most Great Peace shall come.
        The final cleansing.
        The ultimate purification.

The ultimate of sacrifice
in reaching for tomorrow.
And the future will remember us—
And the future will shed tears for us—
Remembering all the years
of the Most Great Suffering.

See The People

See the people
   Endless people
      We the people
         All going
            All wanting
               All needing.
Hear their cries:
   Take me!
      Want me!
         Love me!
            Make me!
Sad people
   Happy people
      All worrying
         All desiring
            Desiring nothing.
Let's get educated!
   Let's make a living
      And above all
         Let's be—practical—logical—reasonable.
God help us!
   God need us!
      What is God?
         God is dead.
No one to hear:
   Their cries
      Our cries
         My cries
Take me
   Want me
      Love me
         Make me!

❧ Hide and Seek

Listen, my children
For I must tell
Why the world
Is going to hell.
We've polluted the waters
And raped the soil,
And now the world
Is out of oil.
Our food is depleted,
We've run out of gas;
There's not enough paper
To wipe your sweet ass.
Resources saved for
 A final fling:
A glorious war.
The world is playing
"Game of the Week,"
And now it's time
To hide and seek!

‿ *Mental Health Center*

Inpatient, Outpatient, Partial too
Are services we offer you.
We help you heal, make you well,
Replace your pain, remove your hell!
We are trained in what we do
In therapy to counsel you.
Years of work and sacrifice
So you might have a better life.
We will not rest upon our laurels,
We have the temperament; we have the morals.
We'll heal by day, we'll pray at night,
That you, like us, will gain insight!

For we take pride in what we do;
We are the best, the chosen few.
We're here for you when storm clouds gather,
Soon as we get our s—t together!
My fears are growing strong today
That I may kill myself someway.
Staff pretend they're kind to me,
But it's a plot that I can see.
I know there are no other choices,
I hear that from secret voices.
 My patients are not really there,
They are not real, they do not care.
But I will teach them all a trick:
Black magic is what made them sick.
For I'm instructed by the Lord—
He said, "Return back to the ward."
So I'll return, help and assist,
For I am but a therapist!
I seek no glory, praise or cheer—
I'm now Employee of the Year!

Split Personality

It's ever so peculiar
I don't know what to do-
I went to bed an Arab
And woke up as a Jew.
I now recite the Torah
Not knowing where I've been.
The last thing I remember
Is the citing of the Muezzin.
None of this is simple
As you will plainly see-
Now I've double trouble,
For I'm at war with me!
My upper and my lower parts
Are fighting for my middle,
My head and feet cry out defeat-
I want to rid this riddle.
Alas! I cannot seem to find
A hope or a solution-
Should I wear my Yalmuke,
Or continue my ablutions?
The battle raging on in me
Will never cease or pass-
The Arab has diarrhea!
The Jew is full of gas!
It's useless to surrender
And give up in defeat.
The USA supplies me arms,
While Russia gives me feet.
I closed my eyes and went to bed
To end this dreadful day.
I woke up an Englishman,
And joined the IRA.

～ Farewell, Joe

Mind-expanding Joe
Sought a way to find
Altered States of Consciousness
To magnify his mind.
LSD and STP
Were his humble start.
He felt his mind expanding
With each murmur of his heart.
First he shot speed,
Then he shot snow.
While shooting Belladonna,
He chewed off his big toe.
He finally reached his limit,
One last trip to try—
Tannic Acid in a needle
Injected in the eye.
He saw multi-polka dots,
No color did he lack—
Then he saw forever
Paisley shades of black.
He sighed aloud, then hanged himself
With a coil of rope.
But no one found his body—
All they found was dope.
His mother and his father
Sadly left the spot
Praying that his soul
Would not go to pot.
They went to church to pray for Joe
At the sacred, solemn mass—
And the incense that was burning
Filled the hall with fumes of grass.
Goodbye Joe, I'll miss you.
Thanks for buying Shit from me.

I'd like to sell the world some Coke
To keep you company.
It's The Real Thing!

God's Garden

The flowers in God's garden
Are many different hues,
From shades of white to brightest red,
With yellows, greens, and blues.
How sadly uninspiring
If each one looked the same,
And every flower planted
Shared a common name.
Each flower bears a fragrance
That is uniquely sweet,
And blends to make the garden
Aromatically complete.
The people in God's garden
Have many facets too.
Fat or thin, rich or poor,
Islamic, Christian, Jew.
So why not take a lesson
From the Gardener's hand
And learn to live in harmony
So all can understand?
God's love is not a secret.
It's etched on every face.
The People Garden is but one:
The blooming human race.

Robert Kogan and Mary Sullivan

 War

The cry of war was in the air.
I heard its horrid sound—
The women screamed, the children cried;
The men fought hard, and still they died.
I rode up to see the front.
The shells fell all around.
"Get down, you blasted fool!" I heard—
The world spun 'round—up rose the ground,
Then silence was the only sound.
I could not speak a word.
When all had cleared I gazed upon
What once had been a field.
Now trampled mud all drenched with blood
Was all that it would yield.
I turned around and then I saw
What must have been a fantasy—
Arranged in rows, like orchard groves,
Were bodies, three by three,
That extended to Infinity
Something only the damned should see.
I gaped and tried to comprehend
Just what this sight could mean,
And standing there I said a prayer
Asking God to change the scene.
And while I stood, there came a man—
At least he seemed to be.
His eyes were red, and on his head
Was written, "War Has Conquered Thee!"
The Spirit of War approached me:
His finger motioned, "Come!"
I could not fight! My soul grew numb!
I had to go; he ordered me.
He took me to his kingdom
And showed me his domain.

He told me of the future,
And all that it would bring.
"Sit down," he said, "and I will show
You sights you've never seen."
A thousand wars passed by my eyes;
A thousand wars that prophesized
Horrors unforeseen.
All the bodies that were there
Were men who died in war.
And like a tree that cast a seed,
Death planted them to do a deed:
Each was to be a war!
Each man who died would represent
Another war to be;
Then countless more would pass away
Until at last would come the day
When life on Earth would cease to be!
Then all went black. I never knew
How long I stayed that way.
I dreamed a thousand dreams of death
And woke the following day.

Having Needs Met

Maslow claims the needs of man
Depend on prior needs
And each fulfillment often brings
Another need to seed.

Horney, in her simple way,
Is anxious to describe
The neurotic core in every man
That motivates his every drive.

And Freud, the Master of them all,
Has cast on man a hex
For every thought and every need
And even man's most pious deed
Is disguised by lust for sex.

I have little else to add
Except a simple creed:
To me the greatest need of all
Is the human need to need.

A Theory of Modern Neurosis

When man descended from the trees
He stood erect and lost his fleas.
For generations after that
He wondered where his fleas were at.
We attained a noble niche
But, in the process, lost our itch.
The need to scratch and halitosis
Developed into our neurosis.
The cure is simple, if you please—
You must return to climbing trees.

Then bend your knees,
And scratch them fleas!

Robert E. and Linda Kogan

ᴄ⁓ *Correspondence with Emily*

INTRODUCTION

The vast majority of Emily Dickinson's (1830-1886) poetry was discovered after her death. During her lifetime, it appears only seven of her poems were published, without her permission and with considerable editorial revisions. Her sister found 1,775 of her poems in a bureau drawer, and others were discovered in old letters she had written to her friends. Her poetry continued to be published from 1890 to 1955.

Not too long ago, while looking over my scrapbook, I discovered some correspondence from Emily, and some poems I sent in reply.

Life's Trades

Dear Robert,

It's such a little thing to weep,
So short a thing to sigh
And yet by trades the size of these
We men and women die!

Love, Emily

⁓

Dear Emily,

My life is measured out by sighs
And from tears I shed.
So I seek comfort from my friends,
Both the living, and the dead!

Love, Robert

Parting

Dear Robert,

My life closed twice before its close,
It yet remains to see
If Immortality unveil
A third event to me,

So huge, so hopeless to conceive,
As these that twice befell
Parting is all we know of heaven,
And all we need of hell.

Love, Emily

Dear Emily,

Of all the sounds that I have heard,
The ones I most deplore
Are footsteps from departing friends—
The closing of the door.

And your door closed before we met
To share our poetry.
But I find comfort in your words—
They keep me company.

Love, Robert

Griefs

Dear Robert,

I measure every grief I meet
With analytic eyes;
I wonder if it weighs like mine,
Or has an easier size.

I wonder if they bore it long,
Or did it just begin?
I could not tell the date of mine,
It feels so old a pain.

I wonder if it hurts to live,
And if they have to try,
And whether, could they choose between,
They would not rather die.

I wonder if when years have piled—
Some thousands—on the cause
Of early hurt, if such a lapse
Could give them any pause;

Or would thy go on aching still
Through centuries above,
Enlightened to a larger pain
By contrast with the love.

The grieved are many, I am told;
The reason deeper lies,—
Death is but one and comes but once,
And only nails the eyes.

There 's grief of want, and grief of cold—
A sort they call 'despair;'
There 's banishment from native eyes,
In sight of native air.

And though I may not guess the kind
Correctly, yet to me
A piercing comfort it affords
In passing Calvary,

To note the fashions of the cross,
Of those that stand alone,
Still fascinated to presume
That some are like my own.

Love, Emily

Dear Emily,

Your grief is but a friend of mine,
For I have known her well.
She rests within my mind,
And makes my life a living hell.

Tis said that time will heal all wounds—
And remove my sorrow,
Yet she resides within the rooms
I'll enter in tomorrow.

I doubt that she would choose to leave.
She's found a friend in me.
Her solitary purpose is
To keep me company.

And when I choose to take my leave
And bid a found farewell,
I fear that she will follow me
To heaven or to hell.

And much like Love, she'll stay with me.
Always by my side.
For throughout all eternity
She'll try be my bride.

If death can come but only once,
Then let it be my fate
To find your soul waiting there
To join and be my mate.
The grief of want and grief of cold
Will always seek to reign.
Yet when your grief has merged with mine,

We will ignore the pain.

So wait for just a little while
Until we can commune
And share our souls through poetry,
For I am coming soon.

Love, Robert

Dear Robert,

Heart, we will forget him!
You and I, to-night!
You may forget the warmth he gave,
I will forget the light.

When you have done, pray tell me,
That I my thoughts may dim;
Haste! lest while you're lagging,
I may remember him!

Love, Emily

Dear Emily,

It's easy to forget
A heart consumed by flame.
Experience is what's left
Once you forget his name.

The heat will dim when thoughts of him
Belong to yesterday.
It may take years to dry your tears,
Before they fade away.

Love, Robert

Dear Robert,

So proud she was to die
It made us all ashamed
That what we cherished, so unknown
To her desire seemed.

So satisfied to go
Where none of us should be,
Immediately, that anguish stooped
Almost to jealousy.

Love, Emily

Dear Emily,

No need to cherish death.
So why seek martyrdom?
When all you have to do is live,
For death will surely come.

Be jealous of the living,
And of the life they led.
Celebrate each new tomorrow
When praying for the dead.

Love, Robert

~ Walter Benton's Poetry

My poetry will never equal that of Benton's.
Will never be able to paint you
As he painted Lillian.
He painted her at dawn,
While she lay sleeping.
He painted her at night,
Painted his gift of sight.
He painted her in all her splendor—
Painted her with love all night long.
My poetry will never equal that of Benton's,
For I must write,
instead of painting every night.

～ To Roger White

INTRODUCTION:

Roger White died in the early 1990's. Around 1996, at least a half a dozen people wrote and told me how similar Roger's poetry was to mine. I could find only two books by Roger, but their impact on me cannot be measured. I started writing when I was 15 years old; and now, years later, when I read Roger; I saw thoughts and feelings I had experienced in the past-reflected back to me through his writings.

Roger, I loved you
Long before I knew you lived
 and we would never have a chance to meet—
  listening to your music while sitting at your feet.
Long before I read a word you wrote
Your words, like music did not die
I now find comfort in your melodies-
They caress the Haifa of my mind.

It is here, we spend a day and night together,
Sharing hope and promises yet to come.
You took the hate, mistrust, and anger,
 the senseless Fkillings that we wear,
 and cleansed the evil stains that clothed us
 released hidden beauty that was there,
 tossed them to the wind—into the air.

I dreamed your words when I was young,
Assuring me that I was not alone, and that you care.
Your gentle words reside within me,
And I am not alone, for you are there.

To John

Sometimes a soul lingers here on earth
Before joining the Heavenly Concourse,
To remain as a Divine Gift.
It ignites the nobility within us;
Take us to poems, prayers and promises.

A part of this soul resides within us as a melody—
    A testimony to love what we feel,
    And feel what we love.
And their art, music and poetry contain the
    Very essence of their soul.

Dear John, each day I hear your song
    And I know you are not gone,
For I feel your soul inside of me.
    And dwell within your symphony.
When I walk, you walk with me.

~ Life, Nature, Hope and Death ~

⤳ The Dance

The circle widens every day
Where spirits dance and shadows play
And in my heart I felt them say
Dance with me.

The sound of music fills the air
With laughter and a joyous prayer
And I no longer feel despair
Inside of me.

For in my youth I tried to dance
But every time I took a chance
I cried out pleading for romance
To stay with me!

But now the circle's calling me
And I shall find my destiny
To join the dance that beckons me
Caress me!

The circle widens every day
The shadows lead me to the way
The enter where my soul can play
For now it's free!
Come dance with me!

❧ *Yesterways*

My mind still lives in yesterdays,
Clinging to my yesterways.

Look within, ignite the fire—
Happy Birthday to desire.

It doesn't hurt to give a hug,
And then retreat and pull the plug.
See the poet searching after:
Inside crying, outside laughter.

If I could see beyond the sea,
I would discover more of me.

Some seek ribbons, others change.
Others seek beyond their range.

Even in the Winter
You are a fresh summer breeze,
        a sandy beach
        a chocolate bar
        a carrousel
Making people happy,
even though the music
creates a melancholy sound.

Creating myths of yesterdays,
Living in my yesterways.

❧ Insanity: A guided tour

I saw a blank, empty face
Radiate a youthful grace.
Her eyes stared but could not see—
Her empty mind cried out to me.

I forced a smile for her to see—
Yet her smile came so naturally!
A simple child, so very pure
That only God could touch or cure.

Afraid to ask or get involved,
The tour moved on, my guilt was solved.
A nameless face on a faceless ward
Continued to smile and talk with the Lord.

Fallen Angel

He stood on the threshold
Of the Altar of Life
In silent meditation,
Thought of the innocence of youth.

She was young, and soft,
And could only
    smile and laugh
    and look and love
    and give—
For a mirror can only reflect what is.

When she returned
Her youth was gone;
    molded now in beauty, charm and grace
    innocence gone in eyes and face
    and could only
    look and love
    and give—
For a mirror must reflect what is.

And from the top
Of the Altar of Life
He removed her picture;
    And he cried out in agony,
    I must blot out reality.
    Then drew upon her pastel eyes
    Tears of youth that symbolize
        the sadness of a fallen angel—
A painting reflects what can be;
A man reflects what might have been.

❧ *The New Creation*

Day One

It was seven years after the time of the End,
And the rains had washed the smell of destruction
Into the heart of the Earth.
Inside the Soul of Man,
The Message,
Silent and dead for so many years
Began to stir and move.
Had this to have happened in the past,
Man would have felt a surge of feelings within him—
Joy! Wonder! Awe! Love!
But hope was left behind in the ashes of the cities,
And only a scattered few felt the warmth
Of the first ray of sunlight.
Others went deeper into the caves,
Unaware that this was not to be another day of fire.
The Soul of Man began to move,
The Letters spoke *The Message,*
And the evening and the morning were the first day.

❧

Day Two

Somewhere in the long forgotten past
The breeze of memory
   of what once was and might have been,
Like gentle hands lifting life from the womb of darkness,
Guided and pushed man through The Valley of Search.
Three days' travel from his cave,
Man again discovers the green of a leaf and a blade of grass,
   and cultivates it into a garden of love.
Something intrinsic—the Soul of Man—reacts
   and places value on green.
This time as a symbol of life and birth.
And at this moment of time, the greatest need of man is man.
Clinging desperately to each other.
The Soul of Man is still afraid of tomorrow.
And in His final longing to forget the pain of the past,
He discovers the pain of today.
And the evening and the morning were the second day.

Day Three

The great Council Hall was empty,
   and the massive gate
   connecting the twin pillars
   awaited the coming of the Tribunal.
The Soul of Man,
   caretaker and protector of the Hall,
   walked the empty corridors
   igniting incense of wisdom.
The building itself was so arranged
    that the rays of the sun would constantly fall
    on the nine paintings of the Year of Destruction.
All who entered the Hall paid homage
   and felt the warmth of Justice and Peace
     captured so vividly
       in the painting
         of the beginning
           of the end
             of the beginning.
When the Tribunal entered, its first formal act
   was to take the Vow of Ignorance.
The Soul of Man rejoiced and cried,
   for He had witnessed an act of knowledge.
And the evening and the morning were the third day.

Day Four

High above the Great City
  the Soul of Man
  became as one with the mountain.
Across the bay, the sea of humanity
    in multitude of voices
      suddenly gave melody to the All Glorious.
Never since Creation had all mankind assembled.
Never again would man know
  the feeling of being alone.
The People of Earth discarded their veil of plurality,
and the Shrine rested on the carpet of Oneness.
The Soul of Man suddenly realized
  the greatest mistake of the past.
    If man is to enter the Valley of Unity,
      he must do it together!
And the evening and the morning were the fourth day.

Day Five

It was the beginning of the Season of Rapture,
And the winds of divine contentment
   caressed the Fruits of the Earth.
The Soul of Man looked deep into the fountain,
And the myriad of reflections
   gave testimony to the new creation.
He felt the presence of the room,
  and so strongly did it speak
    of the fulfillment
      of love and want and need
        that time itself was captured and discarded.
The Soul of Man awaited
  his return to the Universe,
    mindful of the fact that in yesterdays
     man had reached for the stars,
      and in his eagerness
        forgot to tend the meadows.
And the evening and the morning were the fifth day.

Day Six

The Consultation Chamber of every House
   instantly received visual transmission
   from the depths of the Universe,
   enabling all mankind
   to behold the wonders of space
   and travel from astonishment to astonishment.
The Soul of Man left the House and the city
   and crossed the meadow
   and the sea
   breathing the air of creation
   and touching the wonderment of life.
He stopped to watch the children play,
   and became as one with the distant travelers;
   discovering the secrets and mysteries
   of the many Worlds of God.
And the evening and the morning were the sixth day.

Day Seven

The Soul of Man returned
  to the caves from whence he came.
  tilling the soil of the fields
  and planting deep the seeds
  of the remnants
  of the Golden Age of Man
Since the beginning
  that has no beginning
    man has harvested
    the Wealth of Poverty
    the Diversity of Oneness
    and the Birth of Death.
In reaching for the Universe
  and finding that man is not alone,
    The Soul of Man discovered himself,
    And all of creation—
    and the countless million Words of God
      spoke *The Message*
      and trembled at the dawn of infinite unity.
In another time,
in another place,
it was seven years
after the time of the end.
And the evening and the morning were the seventh day.

∾ My Dream

I am a dreamer.
A hopeless, eternal dreamer.
I dream not of what is,
But of what could be.

I dream that Mothers' sons
Will never die in war again,
For on one bright sunny day,
While God was sitting at the Computer of Life,
He deleted hate from all our memory banks.
Prejudice could no longer be accessed,
And all that remained
was an error message within our minds.

I am a dreamer,
A hopeless, eternal dreamer.
I dream not of what is,
But of what should be.

I dream of children everywhere,
Being held and being loved.
CNN no longer has pictures to show
Of children who lie dying on the ground,
Reaching out for help and hope.
Children more bone than flesh,
Who plead for nourishment
As they take their final breath;
But the only one who could offer
Sustenance of milk and bread
Must continue to roll the film
within their camera instead.

I am a dreamer.
A hopeless, eternal dreamer.
I dream not of what is,
But of what may be.

I dream of civil servants
Who are both civil and servants.
They are the rich of the earth,
Who are required to pay
One year of servitude in lieu of tax,
And do so willingly,
For this is their true reward.

I dream that justice will be proclaimed
The Patron Saint of all the courts—in every land.
That killing, rape, and violence
Is an obscure chapter in some forgotten history text.

For I am a dreamer,
A hopeless, eternal dreamer.
I dream not of what is,
But of what must be.

I dream that love and beauty
Are the food we eat,
And all the clothes we wear.
That flowers be declared legal tender,
And "In God We Trust" be embossed on every petal,
And Praise to God be mentioned everywhere.

For I am a dreamer,
A hopeless, eternal dreamer,
I dream not of what is,
But that you share this dream with me.

A Poet's Hat

In the various, assorted classifications of life,
There are many labels I could wear
    that would appeal to me.
One of my favorite selections
    from the wardrobe of sundry roles in life
                    is that of poet.
The word itself implies
form, order, structure, art, music, and sensitivity.
And those who wear it cry out to a sleeping world
That there is something to be said,
    important only to those who choose to listen.
It is a noble label, and should be worn with distinction.
More often than not, it is a self-imposed label,
    and like the *Emperor's New Clothes,*
    known only to its owner—
    while the rest of the world sees only the fool.

I am such a fool.
I do not possess the attributes of a ready–to–wear poet.
I cannot produce greeting card messages
    that ooze with love and Motherhood.
I cannot compose musical notes
    that produce the songs of our times.
I cannot read my words to a waiting guitar,
    strumming through the concert halls of the nation.
All I can do is to mold a word,
    write a sentence,
    illustrate and interpret personal meaning
    to this mad, magnificent, melancholy, marathon
            called Life.

Four Line Poetry

My back grows weak and weary
From burdens that I carry.
And should you ever hear me moan,
It's from the weight of all I own.

Feel the sadness of my mind,
The longing in my soul—
The vastness of the dark.
The empty of a hole.

What will you do when the party is over?
Where will you go when the running is through?
When will you look at yourself in the mirror,
And see that the person you're killing is you.

The ultimate answer
To making man free:
Let's blow up the world
To preserve unity.

Institutes of higher learning
Pave the way to higher earning.
They do little in their role
To nurture or sustain our soul.

I go to bed with empty love
And wrap dry sheets about me.
I waken to my empty self
And wrap dry life around me.

I'd like to offer you the world
And all that you can see,
But all that I am capable

Of giving you—is me.

I want to tear down all the walls
Past memories have built.
Let your pain become a flower—
First fade, then softly wilt.

Ashes to ashes,
Love to dust,
All because
Of lack of rust

The Church is open
To help the Sinner
By making him
A bingo winner!

❧ Taps

The day passes quickly
And once again I can create,
To the mold darkness
Into a thing of beauty.
When alone with my thoughts
I span the sea of time,
To blend the past and present
Into a harmony of perfection.

All wants are fulfilled,
The cool summer breeze
Blows softly through your hair
And youth and innocence reign.
The past no longer exists
And only you and I now share its purity.
We are together
With only the stars and moon
To light our pathway.

❧ The Child Within

When life seems more than you can bear
And all you feel is dark despair,
When you find problems everywhere,
And pain and hurt seems so unfair
       Seek the child within.

If you alone must face the black
For all your friends have turned their back,
They don't have time for you to share
And no one seems to really care,
       Seek the child within.

When life demands you toil all day
And you must work your life away,
There is no time to rest or play
And hope seems lost and far away,
       Seek the child within.

Remember when you laughed and smiled?
Seek within and find that child.
The times of wonder and discover
When tears were wiped away by Mother.

A time of jam and peanut butter
A time for sharing with another.
Carousels and laughing clowns,
Painted nose and painted frowns.
New games to play week after week,
First go hide, and then go seek!
And while seeking, look within,
Let the child come out again!

The child within is safe and pure.
Allows a peace that will endure.
If today brings only sorrow,
Have Faith the sun will shine tomorrow.

Close your eyes and think of when
You were just a child again,
Where hope and promises were fresh and new,
The child within is still with you!

～ Clouds

I look upon a clear blue sky
Rippled clouds go floating by.
They seem to put my mind at rest
And I see nature at its best.

Man–made things I cannot see.
They signify not a thing to me.
Instead there comes from deep within
Sweet music of a violin.
Music played so soft and clear—
Sounds so pure that few can hear.

The music that's inside of me
Unites and forms a symphony.
And when it stops again I see
Visions of reality—
        I see the world again.
But I don't care what comes my way
Because I know there will be a day
        I'll hear that music played again.

~ Mirror Images

Each morning gazing absent–mindedly
Into the mirror I hold in front of me,
I wonder: Who is that old man I see,
Dark circled eyes looking back at me.

He looks so tired, what little hair is gray,
Symbolic, perhaps, a life in disarray.
Easily I recall another day
When a small boy stared before his play,
And asked that I join him.
Feels like only yesterday.

What happened to that nice young man
Preparing for his first dream date?
Wondering would this be the night—
Afraid to even anticipate.
Should he try to kiss her?
Would she kiss him back?
Would she laugh when he said *I love You*?
Should he even try, or just let go
Of just another fantasy
More delusions of his adequacy!

And where is the man I would greet each day,
Before we left to work and earn our pay,
And face new challenges throughout the day.
Those times now seem so far away.
That poor old man I see looked right at me—
Has he always been there—but I refused to see
That he was waiting for a day when I would be
Just like him, anticipating our joint destiny—
Each of us, awaiting anxiously—

What images tomorrow shall we see—
Or shall we just stare, looking endlessly,
Awaiting our final ascendancy—
Together, throughout all eternity.

~ *My Search*

Leaving childhood, I felt as most boys do.
Questioning all there was to see
Doubting everyone, doubting me!
There must be a purpose to reality.
Watching life and people grow
I felt a sudden need to know
Why it was I came to be.

In my youth, I questioned truth.
I searched for wisdom's light
Sought knowledge in the night.

When I began to be a man
Search was sealed within a seal
For toys and joys belong to boys
But a man must never feel.

And now that I am out of breath
And fast approaching rest and death,
Again I wonder what must be
The purpose of reality?
Is life, life? To me it seems
Hard to distinguish life from dreams.

Did I live, or am I dead?
Something needed to be said!
Whatever was I searching for?
It must have been important—whatever was my quest;
I feel a cold wind by the door,
It's time to close my eyes—and rest.

❧ My Soul

There are times I try to paint my soul,
Expose it to the elements.
But oftentimes all I can see
    is an empty canvas!
Perhaps that empty canvas
    is my greatest work of art,
Waiting for the artist's brush,
Waiting to be filled with poetry.

～ The Iceberg

The iceberg silently approaches.
Death wears many masks
And attracts, like a flame to a moth,
Seeking to embrace and betroth.
Majestic and gigantic,
Caressing the Titanic
Without revenge or wrath.
A thing of beauty.
She too will also die.
Merge and melt and rest upon the seabed.
As ice and ship become the newlywed.
Ocean absorbs the living and the dead.

∼ Checkmate

Blackening sky and flashing clouds
Portend the coming of the storm.
The once-calm river dons a shroud
Of angry waves with white-capped thorns.
In fierce crescendo, cannons roar
They blind the fearsome eve
A sable flash engulfs the shore
As Nature's wrath displays her might.
Meek and humble, man stands by
But no one moves the pawn.
"Checkmate!" cries the knowing sky.
The storm has come and gone.

A Spectrum of Time

I listen to the silence.
Whispers of the past
Echo a symphony of time.
And I, the Composer, admire
The harmony of events;
And I, the critic, detect
The discords of mistakes.
The music fades softly into the night.
I peer into the darkness.
Shadows of the future
Rehearse a play of life.
And I, the observer, await the final act
Before judging its merits;
And I, the actor, strive for perfection
Regardless of the unexpected.
The curtain of destiny rises on another act.
I touch the empty canvas.
I feel the portrait of my present.
I, the subject, cannot escape
The frame that surrounds me;
And I, the artist, chose the colors
From an unlimited palette
To paint this spectrum of time.

❧ Finding God

When I first found God
My Soul began to sing
A Nightingale in paradise
The promise of the spring.

My soul began to sing
The Winter passed me by
The promise of the spring
Made my spirit fly.

The Winter passed me by
The Spring winds came to me
Made my spirits fly
My eyes could finally see.

The Springs winds came to me
I felt his loving grace
My eyes could finally see
The beauty of His face.

I felt His loving grace
And when he looked at me
The beauty of his face
Was all that I could see.

And when He looked at me
I could not help but cry
For all that I could see
Was love within His eye.

∾ *Marmenoul*

An old man down by the sea
Speaks of hope that's meant to be.
He thinks alone yet speaks to me,
And so I listen patiently.
There speaks the fool, so thinks the wise.
Without much thought, I realize
That what he says cannot be true,
So I condemn—yet I dream too.
I've sailed over every sea
And seen 'most every land,
And I tell you it's an evil world.
One I can't understand.
But there's an island far away
That's good, and pure, and whole.
A place that's Heaven here on Earth,
I call it Marmenoul.
My rustic face and grayish hair
Are bloodied with this cursed air;
But in my heart and in my soul
I live–on in Marmenoul.
And someday when the tide is low
And mist is in the air
I'll raise my sails up to the sky
And head due south where it must lie.
I'll turn 'round for a last goodbye—
Then straight ahead my ship will fly.
And through the mist will rise up high
My island reaching towards the sky.
"I've found it, lad!, you'll hear me cry
And there I'll stay until I die."
Old man, I thought, good luck to you.
Strange as it all seems
Here is where your island lies—
A Promised Land you know in dreams.

Your search is all in vain, old man.
You'll never reach your goal.
Yet, every person seeks a place
To call their Marmenoul.

～ Assimilation

I came to you of free choice,
Expecting cultural differences.
Your signs advertise,
"Where America's Day Begins"
As if the Pacific offered
The promise of a new beginning.
Before I came I never thought to ask,
"Which America?"
I did not understand that when we came
We came as foreigners.
This is neither judgment nor disappointment,
Just another aspect of reality.
Why should it surprise me that I,
Who reject the wrongs of my heritage,
Bring with me, duty free,
The essence of my heritage?
Letting go will be difficult
Because I am a foreigner.
What do I see?
I see those who marry beyond the barriers of society
Living here to escape the hate of home.
I see others who want to create a new New York,
Fabricated in their own middle-class image.
I see the military,
Who have no choice.
I see the pseudo-academics,
Pretending that they have a choice.
I see a few who attempt to be
All that they are not.
I see others becoming
More than they could ever be.
I see some who really care
And others only experience rejection.

I see a U.S. ghetto.
I see the walls of work, and anxiously await
The discovery of an island.

～ Observing Life

INTRODUCTION

Over the course of my many years as a Consultant for the Joint Commission on Accreditation of Hospitals, I traveled extensively throughout the United States. On one occasion, during a trip to Guam, I had a rare opportunity to record even the most subtle observations in detail.

Watching people at the airport
 I see the face of Life.
Groups of three, laughing with each other,
With no room for others, quickly hurry by.
Lovely, lonely girl, looking straight ahead;
Eyes fixed, for there is just not enough time to get involved.
Uniformed men with soft packages of tenderness
To give to a selective world.
Their ribbons speak loudly
Of other meaningless metal gifts
They gave to strangers.
Little gray lady in furs
Whose skins did you wear?
To keep you warm?
The children are excited.
They are learning young
That mad motion and rushing
Bring laughter, kisses and presents.
        Tell me, happy child,
        What does stillness bring?
Detached groups look out windows
And see a multitude of people
Leaving their pasts, still fastened safely
To their seat belts on cushions advertised to float.
Elsewhere similar planes drop bombs

instead of people.
Across the concourse, a womanly girl with long, brown hair
Sits upon a hard, tattered chair
And watches strangers passing by.
For one brief moment I share her thoughts
And hope tomorrow she will gaze at eyes, instead of feet.
Finally I too sit and ride the vast sky.
Across the aisle a beautiful black woman smiles at me.
She wears a white hat that blends
With the upper limits of the clouds.
We look down at different worlds
      And see beauty.
Here, above the People Hate,
We share the universe,
And we no longer feel alone.

❧ if

if i were a poet
i would always carry with me
pen and paper to write
my constant observations
and impressions of life
so that words of wisdom
would flow forth
twenty four hours a day

in considering this noble endeavor
i first had to establish a level of significance
through the process of elimination
do i have significant thoughts
do i have thoughts
do i have
do i
do

once this decision was made the only thing left to consider
was content

it was then that i decided to cease writing forever
for in fact there are just so many ways to express
love
tenderness
peace
unity
god
and once said...felt expressed
all that is left
is to be

❧ About the Author
Robert E. Kogan

Robert Kogan retired after spending over 30 years in the field of mental health administration. He was born in Wichita, Kansas in 1937 and moved to Dallas, Texas when he was nine years old. Currently he resides in Norman, Oklahoma.
He is married to Linda Kogan and has two beautiful daughters.

His BA Degree is from Denton State University; his MA Degree is from Goddard College, his Ph.D. Degree is from the University of Beverly Hills.

His poetry appears on many other web pages where he has been honored as Poet of the Week, Poet of the Month and featured "guest poet."

His poetry is written in free verse and in rhyme and centers on the themes of love, life and social commentary.

His poetry has been published in:

The American Bard
The American Poet
The Golden Quill Anthology
Prairie Poet
A.F.P.S. Anthology
The Rambler
The Blair Press
Stars And Stripes
The Doylestown Daily Intelligencer
Orison
Georgian Blue Poetry Anthology, 1996
Poetic Voices Of America, Spring 1999

Printed in the United States
3447